Shapes

Contents

 Look and put the sticker.

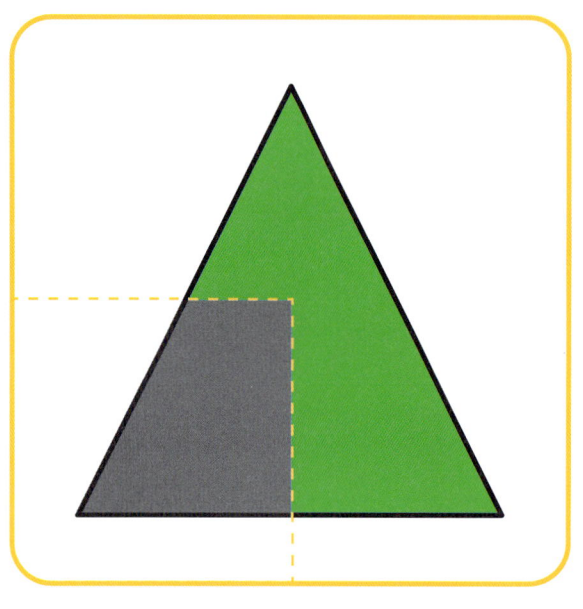

triangle

star

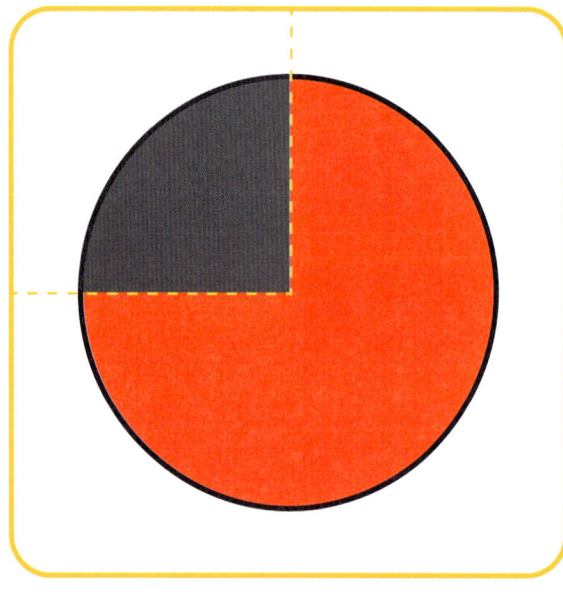

circle

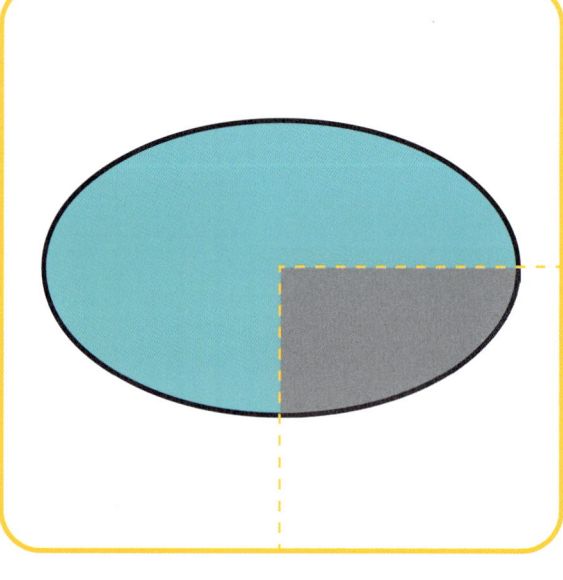

oval

Put sticker on the word.

What shape is it?

It's a [circle] .

Ask and say.

Color and say.

 star

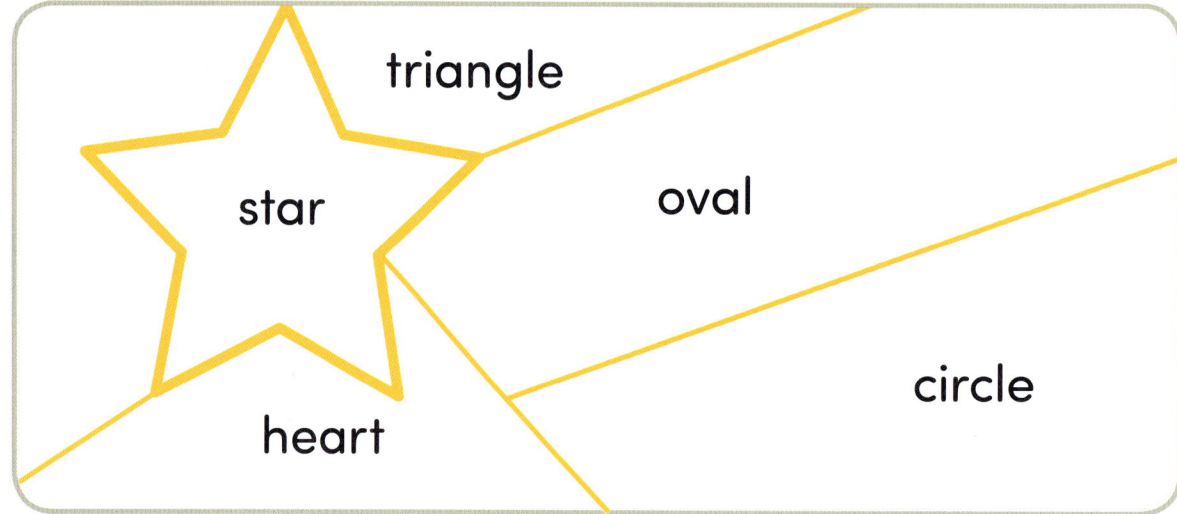

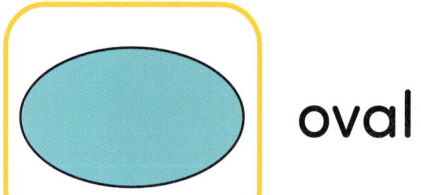 oval

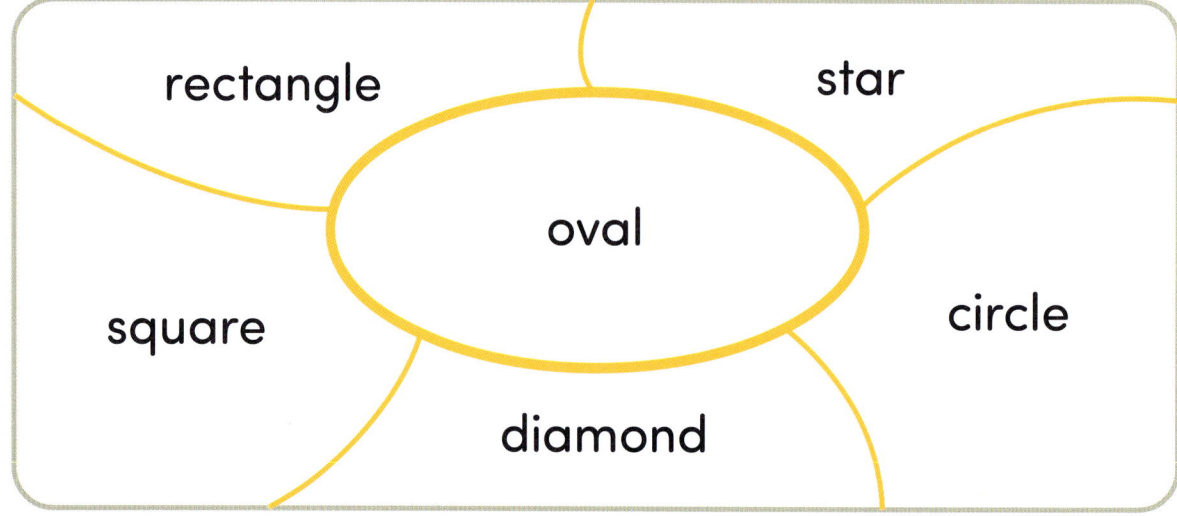

Let's Learn

Sticker

Look and put the sticker.

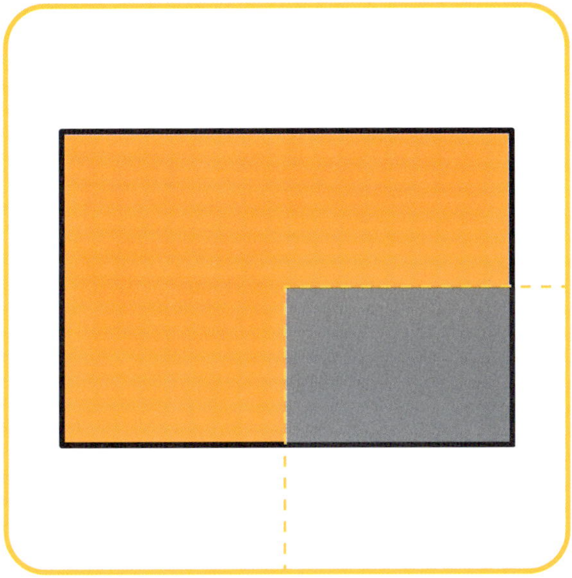

rectangle

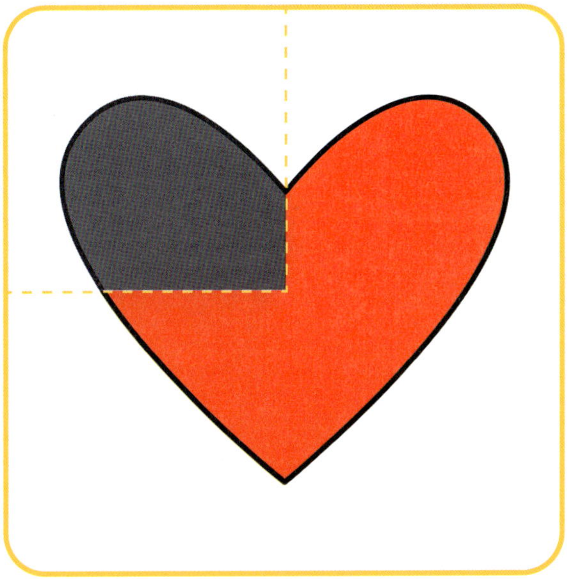

heart

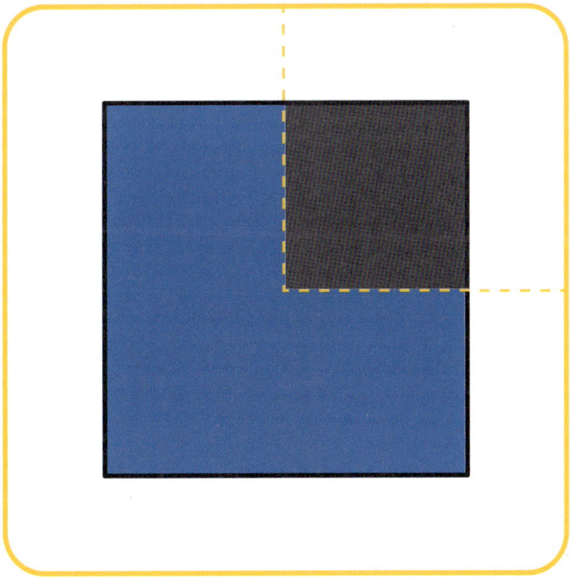

square

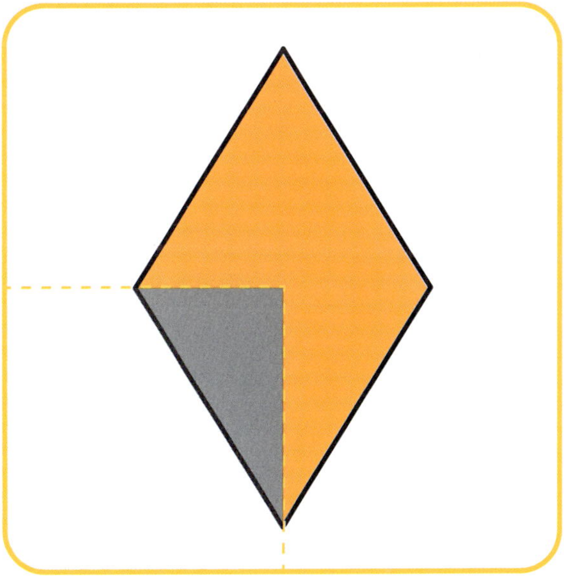

diamond

 **Put sticker on the word.**

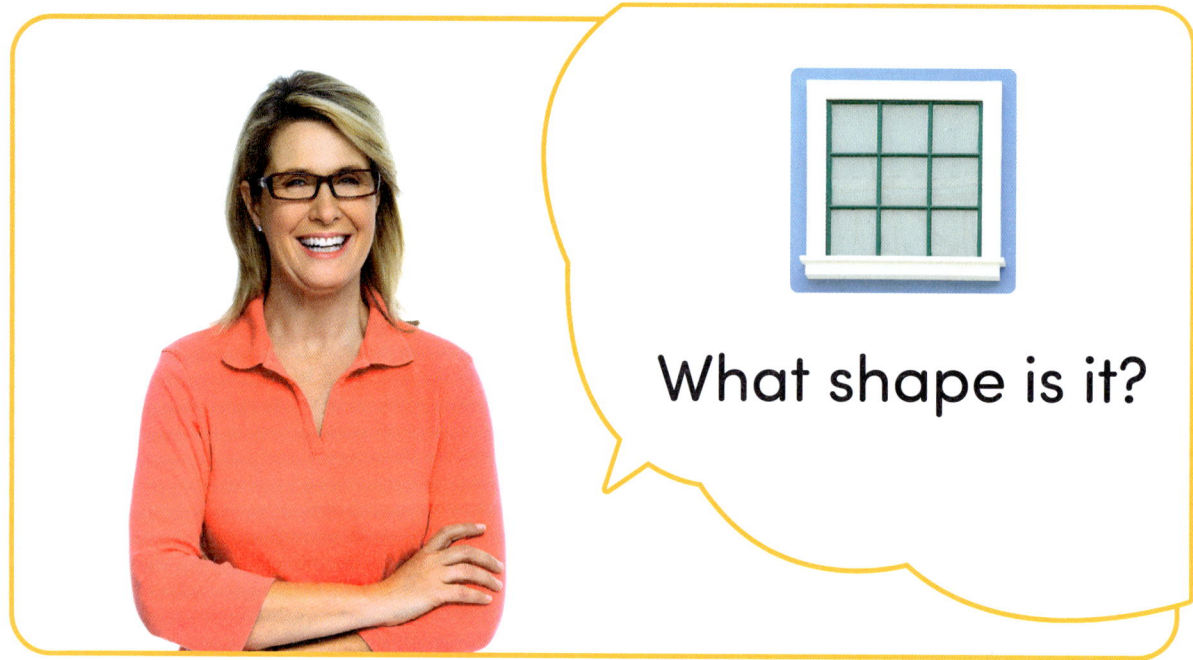

What shape is it?

It's a square .

 Ask and say.

p. 2
p. 3

circle

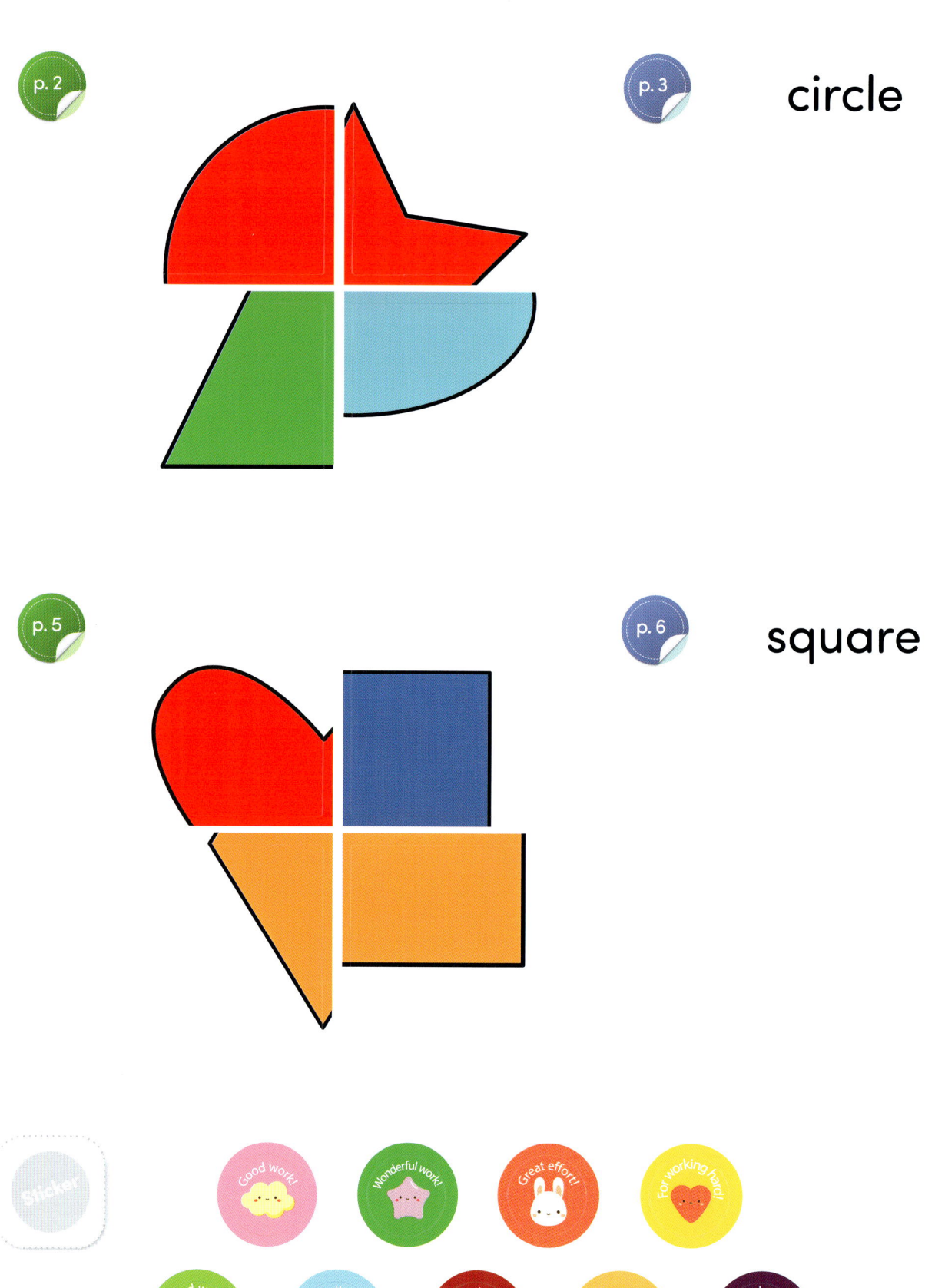

p. 5
p. 6

square

Sticker

Good work!

Wonderful work!

Great effort!

For working hard!

Good work!

Excellent!

Well done!

Well done!

Special award!

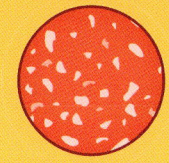

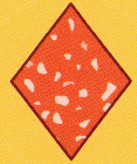

Draw the shape.

triangle

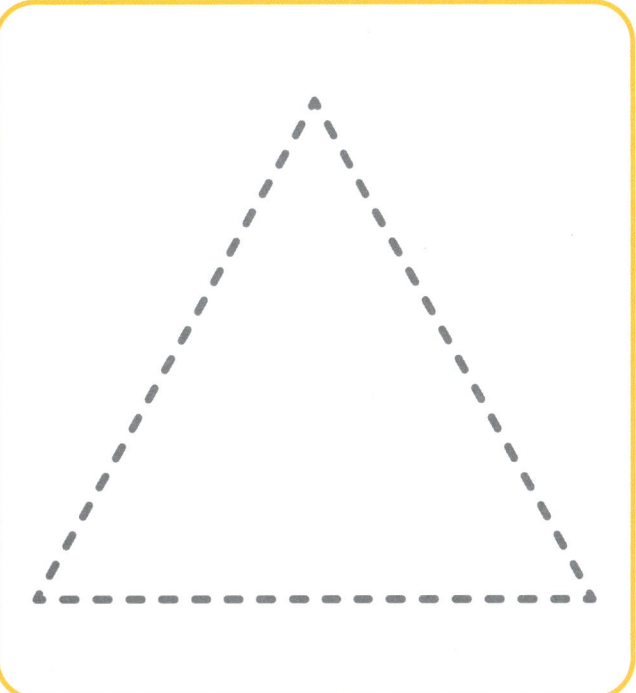

heart

 Make a pizza.

square	circle
rectangle	**triangle**

diamond | star

oval | heart